FIRST 50 SONGS

YOU SHOULD PLAY ON THE XYLOPHONE

Arrangements by Will Rapp

ISBN 978-1-5400-6890-3

Visit Hal Leonard Online at
www.halleonard.com

World headquarters, contact:
Hal Leonard
7777 West Bluemound Road
Milwaukee, WI 53213
Email: info@halleonard.com

In Europe, contact:
Hal Leonard Europe Limited
1 Red Place
London, W1K 6PL
Email: info@halleonardeurope.com

In Australia, contact:
Hal Leonard Australia Pty. Ltd.
4 Lentara Court
Cheltenham, Victoria, 3192 Australia
Email: info@halleonard.com.au

CONTENTS

WHEN THE SAINTS GO MARCHING IN

XYLOPHONE

Traditional

Brightly, in 2

GOD BLESS AMERICA®

XYLOPHPONE

Words and Music by
IRVING BERLIN

Moderately

EVERYTHING'S COMING UP ROSES

from GYPSY

XYLOPHONE

Lyrics by STEPHEN SONDHEIM
Music by JULE STYNE

LET'S GO FLY A KITE

from MARY POPPINS

XYLOPHONE

Words and Music by RICHARD M. SHERMAN
and ROBERT B. SHERMAN

SUPERCALIFRAGILISTICEXPIALIDOCIOUS

from MARY POPPINS

Xylophone

Words and Music by RICHARD M. SHERMAN
and ROBERT B. SHERMAN

CAMPTOWN RACES

XYLOPHONE

Words and Music by
STEPHEN C. FOSTER

SWANEE

XYLOPHONE

Words by IRVING CAESAR
Music by GEORGE GERSHWIN

Broadway style, in 2

13

ZIP-A-DEE-DOO-DAH
from SONG OF THE SOUTH

XYLOPHONE

Music by ALLIE WRUBEL
Words by RAY GILBERT

THE SURREY WITH THE FRINGE ON TOP

from OKLAHOMA!

XYLOPHONE

Lyrics by OSCAR HAMMERSTEIN II
Music by RICHARD RODGERS

WHEN JOHNNY COMES MARCHING HOME

XYLOPHONE

Words and Music by
PATRICK SARSFIELD GILMORE

Moderately, in 2

PUT ON A HAPPY FACE

from BYE BYE BIRDIE

XYLOPHONE

Lyric by LEE ADAMS
Music by CHARLES STROUSE

GAME OF THRONES

Theme from the HBO Series GAME OF THRONES

XYLOPHONE

By RAMIN DJAWADI

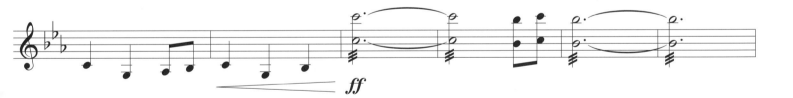

MISSION: IMPOSSIBLE THEME

from the Paramount Television Series MISSION: IMPOSSIBLE

XYLOPHONE

By LALO SCHIFRIN

THE RAINBOW CONNECTION

from THE MUPPET MOVIE

XYLOPHONE

Words and Music by PAUL WILLIAMS
and KENNETH L. ASCHER

IT'S A SMALL WORLD

from Disney Parks' "it's a small world" attraction

XYLOPHONE

Words and Music by RICHARD M. SHERMAN
and ROBERT B. SHERMAN

Moderately

HE'S A PIRATE

from PIRATES OF THE CARIBBEAN: THE CURSE OF THE BLACK PEARL

XYLOPHONE

Written by HANS ZIMMER,
KLAUS BADELT and GEOFF ZANELLI

SHAKE IT OFF

XYLOPHONE

Words and Music by TAYLOR SWIFT,
MAX MARTIN and SHELLBACK

ROLLING IN THE DEEP

XYLOPHONE

Words and Music by ADELE ADKINS
and PAUL EPWORTH

29

MY CHERIE AMOUR

XYLOPHONE

Words and Music by STEVIE WONDER,
SYLVIA MOY and HENRY COSBY

SKATING

XYLOPHONE

By VINCE GUARALDI

CHIM CHIM CHER-EE

from MARY POPPINS

XYLOPHONE

Words and Music by RICHARD M. SHERMAN
and ROBERT B. SHERMAN

LISTEN TO THE MOCKING BIRD

XYLOPHONE

Words by ALICE HAWTHORNE
Music by RICHARD MILBURN

Bluegrass style

FEVER

XYLOPHONE

Words and Music by JOHN DAVENPORT
and EDDIE COOLEY

I'M A BELIEVER

XYLOPHONE

Words and Music by
NEIL DIAMOND

MISIRLOU

XYLOPHONE

Words by FRED WISE, MILTON LEEDS,
JOSE PIÑA and SIDNEY RUSSELL
Music by NICOLAS ROUBANIS

GOD ONLY KNOWS

XYLOPHONE

Words and Music by BRIAN WILSON
and TONY ASHER

ppp

HEART AND SOUL

from the Paramount Short Subject A SONG IS BORN

XYLOPHONE

Words by FRANK LOESSER
Music by HOAGY CARMICHAEL

A HARD DAY'S NIGHT

XYLOPHONE

Words and Music by JOHN LENNON
and PAUL McCARTNEY

Moderately

THE BEST IS YET TO COME

XYLOPHONE

Music by CY COLEMAN
Lyrics by CAROLYN LEIGH

BILLIE JEAN

XYLOPHONE

Words and Music by
MICHAEL JACKSON

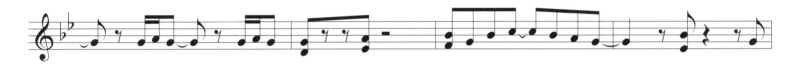

WILLIAM TELL OVERTURE

XYLOPHONE

By GIOACHINO ROSSINI

THE HUSTLE

XYLOPHONE

Words and Music by
VAN McCOY

GRAZING IN THE GRASS

XYLOPHONE

Words by HARRY ELSTON
Music by PHILEMON HOU

SLAVONIC DANCE #1

XYLOPHONE

By ANTONÍN DVOŘÁK
Op. 46, No. 1

61

TURKEY IN THE STRAW

XYLOPHONE

American Folksong

Hoedown feel

DANCING QUEEN

XYLOPHONE

Words and Music by BENNY ANDERSSON,
BJÖRN ULVAEUS and STIG ANDERSON

ROAR

XYLOPHONE

Words and Music by KATIE PERRY,
MAX MARTIN, DR. LUKE,
BONNIE McKEE and HENRY WALTER

Moderately

STAR WARS
(Main Theme)
from STAR WARS: A NEW HOPE

Music by JOHN WILLIAMS

XYLOPHONE

LIVE AND LET DIE

from LIVE AND LET DIE

XYLOPHONE

Words and Music by PAUL McCARTNEY
and LINDA McCARTNEY

Reggae feel

Driving

Slowly

Faster

CAN CAN
from ORPHEUS IN THE UNDERWORLD

XYLOPHONE

By JACQUES OFFENBACH

p   *cresc.*

f

p ——————————————————— *f*   *p*

f

accel.   *ff*

RUSSIAN SAILOR'S DANCE

XYLOPHONE

By REINHOLD GLIERE

THE IRISH WASHERWOMAN

XYLOPHONE

Irish Folksong

Lively, in 2

Faster

Faster still

THE AMERICAN PATROL

XYLOPHONE

By F. W. MEACHAM

Faster

OH! SUSANNA

XYLOPHONE

Words and Music by
STEPHEN C. FOSTER

BUTTONS AND BOWS
from the Paramount Picture THE PALEFACE

XYLOPHONE

Words and Music by JAY LIVINGSTON
and RAY EVANS

TICO TICO
(Tico Tico No Fuba)

XYLOPHONE

Words and Music by ZEQUINHA ABREU,
ALOYSIO OLIVEIRA and ERVIN DRAKE

ORANGE BLOSSOM SPECIAL

XYLOPHONE

Words and Music by
ERVIN T. ROUSE

PINE APPLE RAG

XYLOPHONE

By SCOTT JOPLIN

MOLLY ON THE SHORE

XYLOPHONE

By PERCY ALDRIDGE GRAINGER

NOLA

XYLOPHONE

By FELIX ARNDT

Relaxed Two-beat feel

mp

Audio Access Included — HAL•LEONARD EASY INSTRUMENTAL PLAY-ALONG

- Perfect for beginning players
- Carefully edited to include only the notes and rhythms that students learn in the first months playing their instrument
- Great-sounding demonstration and play-along tracks
- Audio tracks can be accessed online for download or streaming, using the unique code inside the book

DISNEY
Book with Online Audio Tracks

The Ballad of Davy Crockett • Can You Feel the Love Tonight • Candle on the Water • I Just Can't Wait to Be King • The Medallion Calls • Mickey Mouse March • Part of Your World • Whistle While You Work • You Can Fly! You Can Fly! You Can Fly! • You'll Be in My Heart (Pop Version).

00122184	Flute	$9.99
00122185	Clarinet	$9.99
00122186	Alto Sax	$9.99
00122187	Tenor Sax	$9.99
00122188	Trumpet	$9.99
00122189	Horn	$9.99
00122190	Trombone	$9.99
00122191	Violin	$9.99
00122192	Viola	$9.99
00122193	Cello	$9.99
00122194	Keyboard Percussion	$9.99

CLASSIC ROCK
Book with Online Audio Tracks

Another One Bites the Dust • Born to Be Wild • Brown Eyed Girl • Dust in the Wind • Every Breath You Take • Fly like an Eagle • I Heard It Through the Grapevine • I Shot the Sheriff • Oye Como Va • Up Around the Bend.

00122195	Flute	$9.99
00122196	Clarinet	$9.99
00122197	Alto Sax	$9.99
00122198	Tenor Sax	$9.99
00122201	Trumpet	$9.99
00122202	Horn	$9.99
00122203	Trombone	$9.99
00122205	Violin	$9.99
00122206	Viola	$9.99
00122207	Cello	$9.99
00122208	Keyboard Percussion	$9.99

CLASSICAL THEMES
Book with Online Audio Tracks

Can Can • Carnival of Venice • Finlandia • Largo from Symphony No. 9 ("New World") • Morning • Musette in D Major • Ode to Joy • Spring • Symphony No. 1 in C Minor, Fourth Movement Excerpt • Trumpet Voluntary.

00123108	Flute	$9.99
00123109	Clarinet	$9.99
00123110	Alto Sax	$9.99
00123111	Tenor Sax	$9.99
00123112	Trumpet	$9.99
00123113	Horn	$9.99
00123114	Trombone	$9.99
00123115	Violin	$9.99
00123116	Viola	$9.99
00123117	Cello	$9.99
00123118	Keyboard Percussion	$9.99

CHRISTMAS CAROLS
Book with Online Audio Tracks

Angels We Have Heard on High • Christ Was Born on Christmas Day • Come, All Ye Shepherds • Come, Thou Long-Expected Jesus • Good Christian Men, Rejoice • Jingle Bells • Jolly Old St. Nicholas • Lo, How a Rose E'er Blooming • On Christmas Night • Up on the Housetop.

00130363	Flute	$9.99
00130364	Clarinet	$9.99
00130365	Alto Sax	$9.99
00130366	Tenor Sax	$9.99
00130367	Trumpet	$9.99
00130368	Horn	$9.99
00130369	Trombone	$9.99
00130370	Violin	$9.99
00130371	Viola	$9.99
00130372	Cello	$9.99
00130373	Keyboard Percussion	$9.99

POP FAVORITES
Book with Online Audio Tracks

Achy Breaky Heart (Don't Tell My Heart) • I'm a Believer • Imagine • Jailhouse Rock • La Bamba • Louie, Louie • Ob-La-Di, Ob-La-Da • Splish Splash • Stand by Me • Yellow Submarine.

00232231	Flute	$9.99
00232232	Clarinet	$9.99
00232233	Alto Sax	$9.99
00232234	Tenor Sax	$9.99
00232235	Trumpet	$9.99
00232236	Horn	$9.99
00232237	Trombone	$9.99
00232238	Violin	$9.99
00232239	Viola	$9.99
00232240	Cello	$9.99
00233296	Keyboard Percussion	$9.99

Disney characters and artwork © Disney Enterprises, Inc.

www.halleonard.com

Prices, content, and availability subject to change without notice.